D0478477

FRONTIER LAND

NATIVE AMERICANS

OF THE FRONTIER

Charles W. Sundling

Visit us at
www.abdopub.com

Published by ABDO Publishing Company, 4940 Viking Drive, Edina, MN 55435.
Copyright ©2000 by Abdo Consulting Group, Inc. International copyrights
reserved in all countries. No part of this book may be reproduced in any form
without written permission from the publisher.

Printed in the United States.

Edited by: Tamara L. Britton
Art Direction: John Hamilton
Contributing Editor: Morgan Hughes

Cover photo: Corbis
Interior photos: Image Club Graphics, pages 1, 3, 5, 7, 9, 11, 15, 17, 19, 21,
                  22, 23, 24, 27, 31
                  Corbis, pages 13, 25, 26, 28

Sources: Adams, Alexander B. *Sunlight and Storm: The Great American West.*
New York: Putnam and Sons, 1977; *American Heritage History of the Great
West, The.* New York: American Heritage, 1965; Ballantine, Betty, and
Ballantine, Ian (editors). *The Native Americans: An Illustrated History.* Atlanta,
1993; Bancroft-Hunt, Norman and Forman, Werner. *The Indians of the Great
Plains.* New York: Peter Bedrick Books, 1981; Brown, Dee. *Bury My Heart At
Wounded Knee.* New York: Henry Holt and Co., 1970; *The Buffalo Hunters.*
Alexandria: Time-Life Books, 1993; Laubin, Reginald & Laubin, Gladys. *The
Indian Tipi.* Norman: University of Oklahoma Press, 1977; Lamar, Howard
(editor). *The Reader's Encyclopedia of the Old West.* New York, 1977; Lowie,
Robert. *The Indians of the Plains.* Lincoln, NE: University of Nebraska Press,
1982; Milner, Clyde A. et. al. (editors). *The Oxford History of the American West.*
New York, 1990.

Library of Congress Cataloging–in–Publication Data

Sundling, Charles W.
    Native Americans of the frontier / Charles W. Sundling
        p. cm. — (Frontier land)
    Includes index.
    Summary: Describes the life and customs of Native American people living on
the Great Plains before the arrival of the white men.
    ISBN 1-57765-042-5
    1. Indians of North America—Great Plains—History—Juvenile literature. 2.
Indians of North America—Great Plains—Social life and customs—Juvenile
literature. [1. Indians of North America—Great Plains] I. Title. II. Series:
Sundling, Charles W. Frontier land.
E78.G73S89 2000
978—DC21   98-5175
                                                  CIP
                                                  AC

CONTENTS

Property of Dexter
Middle School Library

THE GREAT AMERICAN DESERT

In 1803, the United States bought the Louisiana Territory from France. The land stretched from the Mississippi River to the Rocky Mountains, and from Canada to the Gulf of Mexico. Little was known about the area, so President Thomas Jefferson asked Meriwether Lewis and William Clark to explore it. Lewis and Clark traveled the land for more than two years, and when they finally came back they reported that most of the land was uninhabitable.

Almost 20 years later, Army Major Stephen H. Long explored some of the land again. He thought settlers could never live there. He drew a map and named the area the Great American Desert. Today we call it the Great Plains.

Many early settlers stayed away from the Great Plains. The region had few trees and little water. Settlers needed trees for wood to burn for warmth and cooking and to make houses and other buildings. They needed water for their crops and for animals to drink.

The region wasn't useless to others, however. Both the nomadic tribes and the village tribes knew how to live on the Great American Desert. Native Americans loved the land, referring to it as Grandmother, or Mother. The village tribes lived most of the year in small villages and farmed small pieces of land near rivers.

The nomadic tribes lived in tepees and traveled often, seldom staying in one place for very long. Most Western movies and books depict the nomadic tribes. Their members were expert horse riders, skilled warriors, and craftspeople. Native Americans on the Plains depended on animals like bison, often called buffalo, and the land around them.

Although explorers found the Great Plains to be uninhabitable, Native Americans knew how to live on the land.

VILLAGE TRIBES

Three village tribes lived in the northern Great Plains. They were the Mandan, Hidatsa, and Arikara. The Osage, Pawnee, and Omaha lived near the center of the Great Plains. Their neighboring tribes were the Missouri, Kansa, and Iowa.

The traveling, or nomadic, tribes often fought with the village tribes, sometimes to steal their horses. In order to protect their homes, the village tribes preferred to live on high hills or bluffs near rivers. The bluffs had three steep sides, which gave the villages more protection. Many tribes piled dirt walls, called embankments, around their villages. They also made wood barriers, or palisades, which were too high for an attacker to climb over. Native Americans of the village tribes lived in either earth lodges or tepees.

Many Native Americans lived in villages like this one.

The village tribes farmed small plots that were seldom larger than three acres and sometimes as small as one-half acre. (Today Great Plains farmers typically plant hundreds of acres.) Unlike most of today's farmers, the Native American farmers were usually women. While the village tribes often planted beans, squash, pumpkins, and sunflowers, their most important crop was maize, the ancestor of modern corn.

Like all farmers, Native Americans had trouble farming. Since they had no plows to break the hard dirt, they used buffalo or elk shoulder bones for hoes and rakes. However, the bones broke easily. They also had no trained, or draft, animals to help them. With no plows, strong tools, or draft animals, they were forced to farm the soft land near rivers.

The village tribes usually grew the same crops in the same plots every year. Planting the same crops every year drained the land of nutrients. Worn out land doesn't grow crops very well. Also, they usually didn't fertilize to enrich the soil.

Sometimes millions of grasshoppers came and ate the crops. Sometimes not enough rain fell, and the crops died. If too much rain fell, the crops would drown. Birds or animals could also harm the crops.

Because of all these difficulties, farming seldom gave the village tribes enough to eat. To feed everybody, they also needed to hunt. Like the nomadic tribes, the village tribes mostly hunted buffalo.

NOMADIC TRIBES

Most of the nomadic tribes lived in the western Great Plains. Usually, only their war parties went to the eastern part of the Great Plains. The war parties fought the village tribes and stole their horses.

Some of the nomadic tribes were called the Cheyenne, Arapaho, and Blackfoot. The Crow, Cree, and Sioux (also called Dakota, Nakota, and Lakota) were nomadic tribes, too. These six tribes, along with others, lived in the northern and western parts of the Great Plains. The Comanche and Kiowa were two tribes who traveled in the Great Plains' southern area.

Neither the village tribes nor the nomadic tribes believed people owned land. People, animals, and plants shared the land, but did not own it. Owning land was like owning air. Land, like air, was for everybody to use.

American settlers did not understand this concept. They believed in land ownership, and mistakenly thought Native Americans did too. Owning land was important to American settlers.

Left: *This nomadic tribe is on the move.*

Generally, nomadic tribes stayed in bands, or small groups. The bands moved regularly from place to place. They moved for many reasons, sometimes to follow buffalo herds, or to find fresh grazing land for their horses. Also, they had to move to keep away from enemy tribes.

Native American tribes of the Great Plains.

Horses and dogs were used as pack animals to carry the band's belongings. The bands placed smaller belongings in big rawhide pouches called parfleches, which they strapped to their horses' sides.

Some horses and dogs dragged a type of sled called a travois, which had belongings placed on it. A travois had two poles tied at an animal's shoulders. The ends of the poles extended to the ground behind the animal. A net was stretched between the poles. The band put dried meat, clothes, and tools on the net. Old, sick, or young people sometimes rode on the travois, while the others rode horses.

Many tribes used tepees for shelter, which looked like upside down cones. They were made of buffalo hides and wooden poles. Tepees had plenty of room, and were cool in the summer and warm in the winter. Rain ran off their sides. The tepee's best feature was its ease in moving from place to place.

Some Native Americans painted decorations on their tepees that depicted brave acts. Others painted geometric designs. Many tepees were not decorated at all. The women sewed the buffalo hides together and wrapped them around wooden poles. A fire ring was built on the floor of the tepee, with smoke escaping through a hole at the top. The hole could be closed in bad weather.

When village tribes went hunting, they took tepees to live in. The nomadic tribes lived in tepees all the time. The women of the nomadic tribes assembled the tepees, usually arranging them in a circle or semicircle. It did not take much time for them to put up or take down their tepees.

A CHILD IS THE GREATEST GIFT

The tribes of the Great Plains believed that children were special gifts. The tribes knew that many healthy children meant the tribe would last longer. The Sioux believed children came to worthy people who prayed honestly and regularly, and gave the right sacrifices to the universe's creator. Also, they promised to be good parents.

Life was difficult on the Great Plains. A Native American child needed to be ready for many unpleasant things. At times, there was not enough food. Severe winter weather could make the tepees cold. Enemy tribes sometimes stole belongings or killed family members.

Generally, mothers were in charge of the children. Until she married, a girl obeyed her mother, and until his voice grew deeper, a boy answered to his mother. Mothers took care of the children. Mothers, not fathers, owned the tepees. They also owned the things inside of the tepees.

Native Americans of the Great Plains rarely hit their children. They thought striking a child was bad. Occasionally, a mother had an older brother or an uncle discipline a misbehaving child. Instead of spanking, Native Americans threw water on misbehaving two- or three-year-old children. They also frightened misbehaving children by telling them

This photo of a Navajo papoose (young child) on a cradleboard was taken near Window Rock, Arizona, in 1936. A cradleboard made it easy for a mother to carry her child on her back or prop her child against a tree.

that evil spirits in the shapes of owls or coyotes might take them away.

A mother hugged and fed a crying infant, but if the baby kept crying, she put it in its cradleboard, a carrier made of wood. Then she took the baby away from the camp, hanging the cradleboard on a bush or tree. After the baby stopped crying, they came back to the camp. Mothers did this to keep a tribe's enemies from finding their camp.

Native Americans encouraged their children, and complimented them. A well-behaved child received a tasty treat. A father sang a song of praise for a well-behaved son or daughter.

Relatives or tribal elders usually named children. Girls kept their names all their lives, but many times boys' names changed, usually if they did something brave. A boy's name also changed if he had a special dream or vision.

The most important thing in a Native American's life was to earn the tribe's respect. Native Americans taught their children to think of the tribe. Being brave and tough was useful, but day-to-day life called for treating others well.

When the youngsters grew older, the boys and girls didn't spend as much time together. Older boys learned how to become men, hunters, and warriors. Older girls learned how to become wives, mothers, and workers.

The Sun Dance is a Native American ceremony.

DREAMS UNDER THE SUN

The tribes of the Great Plains were a religious people. Their religious beliefs touched everything in their lives. They said prayers before they hunted, held religious ceremonies before certain activities, and had great faith in dreams or visions.

The Sun Dance was perhaps the Plains tribes' most important ceremony. Most Sun Dance ceremonies were done to renew the tribes' links to the spirit world and the natural world. It was usually held in the middle of summer by the tribes' young men. Before the ceremony, the Sun Dancers ate or drank nothing. Other people in the tribe prepared for the ceremony by building a Sun Dance lodge and gathering special food like buffalo tongue. A special tree, which had to be tall and straight, was cut. The Sun Dancers sharpened sticks, then pushed them through the skin on their chest or back. Leather strips were tied to the sticks and then attached to the special tree.

Men beat on drums as the Sun Dancers moved back from the tree or danced. This pulled on the sticks, which caused great pain, yet they continued. The dancers' hunger, thirst, and pain often caused them to have visions, or hallucinations. The Sun Dance ceremony lasted up to 12 days from the time the tribe began preparing until the end of the ceremony.

The Plains tribes' religious beliefs were very important to them. Each tribe had different beliefs and ceremonies, and passed these beliefs to their children.

This group of Ponca Indians, wearing matching skirts and holding tall banners, gather for the Sun Dance in Oklahoma.

BUFFALO HUNTERS

One American pioneer wrote that he traveled two days to move through a buffalo herd. Another pioneer believed a herd he witnessed to be 30 miles (48 km) wide and 70 miles (113 km) long. Experts don't know exactly how many buffalo once lived on the Great Plains. Some think there were between 15 and 30 million, or even 60 million.

The buffalo were life-givers of the Great Plains Native Americans. In their big bodies the buffalo had almost everything Native Americans needed. Some tribes believed buffalo had a special power in them. They believed that eating buffalo gave them the special power. Before a buffalo hunt, Native Americans blessed the buffalo. They thanked the buffalo for giving their lives to the tribe.

A train waits as a large herd of buffalo blocks the tracks.

Native Americans used buffalo hides for tepees, clothing, and bedding. Warriors used the thickest part of the hide to make shields. Buffalo hair made good rope, stuffing for pillows, and balls for games. Women used buffalo horns and hooves as bowls and spoons. Knives, paintbrushes, and other tools were made from buffalo bones. Native Americans even used the buffalo tails as flyswatters.

For food, Native Americans ate buffalo livers, brains, and bone marrow uncooked. Other parts were boiled in water or roasted over fires. Extra meat was cut or sliced into thin strips. These strips were dried. The dried strips, or jerky, did not rot or spoil for a long time.

Pemmican was another type of treated meat that lasted a long time. The women pounded dried meat and berries into a powder. Then they mixed the powder with fat or bone marrow. Pemmican could be stored and eaten in the winter months.

When a buffalo hunt began, scouts were sent out to search for a herd. When the scouts found buffalo, they reported back to camp. Tribes often picked hunt leaders with a lot of buffalo-hunting experience. They knew which animals were the best to kill, and knew what to do in emergencies, like buffalo stampedes.

Hunting buffalo was quite dangerous. Mature, full-grown male buffalo, called bulls, stood 6 feet (1.8 m) tall. Bulls could weigh around 2,000 pounds (907 kg). Female buffalo, called cows, were smaller but still dangerous.

Native Americans hunted buffalo several different ways. One way was to force a herd to run off a steep hill or cliff. The hunters screamed and waved robes, which frightened the buffalo and caused the herd to run right off a nearby cliff. Unfortunately, this method killed more buffalo than a tribe could use.

Another way Native Americans hunted buffalo was to corral the buffalo into an area where they could be killed easily. The Native Americans would make a fence, or use barriers like canyon walls, on two or three sides of the group and set fire to the remaining sides. The buffalo would run from the fire into the corral, where the hunters could then kill the best animals. Native Americans did not use this

A buffalo hunt could be a very dangerous undertaking, with adult male buffalo weighing around 2,000 pounds (907 kg).

method often, since fence-making material was scarce, and fences took a long time to build. Also, many times frightened buffalo easily broke through the fences.

Native American hunters also stalked buffalo on foot by covering themselves in wolfskin. Then they crawled on hands and knees toward the buffalo. Wolves seldom threatened healthy buffalo, so the buffalo gave little attention to the hunters. This method gave hunters the pick of the best animals to kill.

The hunters' most effective way to hunt buffalo was on horseback. Native Americans were skilled riders. Hunters on horses made a circle around a small group of buffalo that strayed from the herd. Buffalo that split away from the group were easier to kill. The hunters rode among the buffalo and shot their arrows at them. Some hunters stuck lances or spears into the buffalo. Hunters aimed their arrows or spears behind the buffalo's shoulders, hoping to pierce the animal's heart.

An arrow or spear in the heart usually killed a buffalo quickly. A badly wounded animal could run a mile (1.6 km) or more before it died. Also, a wounded buffalo was more likely to attack rather than just run away.

After the hunt, the Native Americans removed the livers from the dead buffalo, then ate them raw. Every part of the buffalo was used.

After forcing a small group of buffalo to split away from the main herd, Native Americans hunted down their quarry on horseback, using arrows and lances for the kill.

THE PLAINS HORSE

Spanish explorers brought horses to the American frontier. At first, there were only a few horses in the new land, but their numbers quickly increased. After a while, horses either escaped or were stolen from the Spanish. Soon horses ran wild on the Great Plains.

Horses greatly changed Native Americans' way of life. Horses were as important as buffalo—in some ways, they were even more important. With horses, tribes could travel great distances. Native Americans also took more belongings with them, made bigger tepees, and killed more buffalo. Wars against other tribes also became deadlier.

Native Americans believed that those with lots of horses were rich. Some tribal leaders owned as many as 200 horses. A young warrior gave horses to his bride's father. A warrior spent many hours on his favorite horse, training it for hunting and battle.

Many times a hunter put feathers, embroidery, or fancy needlework in his hunting ponies' tails or manes. Other hunters painted designs on their favorite horses. Some warriors had the tail and head of a favorite horse put near their burial grounds.

Native Americans obtained horses in many ways. They captured wild horses, called mustangs, and trained them. They traded with other tribes for horses. They also stole horses from other tribes.

Native Americans loved their horses. Horses made their way of life on the Great Plains better.

Native Americans would paint designs on their horses or tie feathers or embroidery in their horses' manes.

This warrior uses his horse as a shield as he gallops past enemy riders.

A TRAIL OF BLOOD

By the 1840s, Native Americans were continually battling with United States soldiers over land. War between them seemed unstoppable. Native Americans lived on land that American pioneers wanted. Native Americans fought to save their families and way of life.

At first, the settlers only wanted trails or wagon roads through the "Great American Desert." They still believed the Great Plains could not be farmed. Only a few settled on the Native Americans' hunting grounds.

The first big movement of settlers were families who wanted to farm land in Oregon and Washington. A second big wave of people traveled through the area in 1849. These people, called "Forty-Niners," were interested in the gold fields of California. They had no interest in staying on the Great Plains.

These American pioneers needed trails, or wagon roads. Native Americans saw the roads as threats. They feared the pioneers because pioneers killed buffalo and brought diseases that killed

At first, white settlers like these only wanted to pass through the "Great American Desert."

As pioneers poured into the Great Plains, Native Americans fought to protect their way of life, and sometimes attacked stagecoaches.

Native Americans. Red Cloud, a great Sioux chief, said that pioneers left a trail of blood behind them. As a result, Native Americans attacked the pioneer travelers. The travelers demanded help, and the United States government built forts to protect the pioneers on their journeys.

In 1851, the Native Americans agreed to the Fort Laramie Treaty. The main purpose of the treaty was to assure safe travel for white settlers along the Oregon Trail from Missouri to Oregon. The United States government promised to leave the Great Plains alone. A few years later, however, war began again. American pioneers now wanted the tribes' land.

The American Civil War (1861-1865) stopped a lot of movement through the Plains. But when the Civil War was over, many pioneers began passing through and settling on the Great Plains. The United States wanted the Native Americans to give up the land peacefully. The government

Lieutenant Colonel George Custer fought and died at the Battle of the Little Bighorn in Wyoming, June 25, 1876.

made many treaties, or agreements, with the tribes. The Native Americans agreed to live in certain areas, which were called reservations. The United States promised to help the Native Americans live on the reservations.

The reservations, however, contained poor farming and hunting land. Sometimes United States soldiers forced tribes to move to the reservations. When Native Americans left the reservations, soldiers forced them to go back.

Property of Dexter
Middle School Library

The fight between government soldiers and the Cheyenne and Lakota of the northern Plains for land lasted many years. The northern tribes' greatest victory was against Lieutenant Colonel George Custer. In 1876, at the Battle of Little Bighorn, Native Americans killed Custer and more than 200 of his soldiers. Other battles followed, but the soldiers eventually conquered the northern tribes.

The tribes of the southern Plains also fought United States soldiers. Soon, the soldiers defeated the Kiowa, Comanche, and Arapaho tribes, then forced them to live on reservations.

The last major fight happened over 100 years ago at Wounded Knee Creek in South Dakota. United States soldiers were guiding 350 Native Americans to a fort. On December 29, 1890, soldiers thought they had been shot at. Many of the soldiers shot back, killing between 150 and 300 men, women, and children. The life that the Native Americans had known on the frontier had come to an end.

This is a scene from the massacre at Wounded Knee.

INTERNET SITES

http://www.state.sd.us/state/executive/tourism/sioux/sioux.htm

This guide to the Great Sioux Nation, put together by the South Dakota Department of Tourism, contains historical and cultural information on the Dakota, Lakota, and Nakota Sioux tribes of the northern Plains.

http://www.heard.org/

The Heard Museum in Phoenix, Arizona, is a private, non-profit museum founded in 1929. This internationally acclaimed museum is one of the best places to experience the many cultures and art of Native Americans of the Southwest. The Web site includes numerous on-line exhibits.

These sites are subject to change. Go to your favorite search engine and type in "Native Americans" for more sites.

PASS IT ON

History buffs: educate readers around the country by passing on information you've learned about Native Americans. Share your little-known facts and interesting stories. We want to hear from you!

To get posted on the ABDO Publishing Company Web site, email us at "History@abdopub.com"

**Visit the ABDO Publishing Company Web site at:
www.abdopub.com**

GLOSSARY

Acre: A unit for measuring the size of a piece of land.

Band: A group of people, or a family unit of Native Americans.

Barrier: A structure, such as a fence, built to stop people or animals.

Bluff: A high or steep hill.

Congress: A group of people who make laws.

Cradleboard: A wooden carrier for babies.

Embankment: A pile of dirt that makes a wall.

Embroidery: Something made with needlework.

Exhaust: To wear out, or use up.

Explore: To search into or travel to find what something is like.

Great American Desert: The Great Plains.

Great Plains: The land from the Rocky Mountains to just west of the Mississippi River, and from the Rio Grande to the delta of the MacKenzie River in Canada.

Incredible: Not believable, amazing.

Lance: A long, round piece of wood with a sharp point at one end.

Maize: The plant modern corn came from.

Marrow: The material inside a bone.

Nomadic: Traveling from place to place.

Pack animal: An animal used to carry things.

Palisades: Fences made of logs with sharp ends.

Parfleche: Leather bag or pouch.

Pemmican: Dried meat and berries that have been pounded into powder and mixed with fat.

Pioneers: People who come into unknown land to settle.

Pouch: A bag.

Reservation: Land to be used only by Native Americans.

Sacrifice: To give up something of great value to another.

Semicircle: Half of a circle.

Settler: People who come to live in a certain area.

Tepee: A movable tent that looks like an upside-down cone and is made of wooden poles with an animal-skin covering.

Travois: A frame hung between wood poles and pulled by a dog or horse and used to carry belongings.

Treaty: An agreement or promise made between people.

Tribe: A large number of groups or bands.

Warrior: A person who fights in battles and wars.

Worthy: Something or somebody that is important or valuable.

Fort Laramie, Wyoming

INDEX